D1606551

TO MAKE

ROOM FOR

THE SEA

Also by Adam Clay

Stranger
A Hotel Lobby at the Edge of the World
The Wash

TO MAKE

ROOM FOR

THE SEA

poems by

ADAM CLAY

MILKWEED EDITIONS

© 2020, Text by Adam Clay
All rights reserved. Except for brief quotations in critical articles or reviews,
no part of this book may be reproduced in any manner without prior written
permission from the publisher: Milkweed Editions, 1011 Washington Avenue
South, Suite 300, Minneapolis, Minnesota 55415.
(800) 520-6455
milkweed.org

Published 2020 by Milkweed Editions
Printed in the United States of America
Cover design by Mary Austin Speaker
Cover artwork: *"a way out" by Susan Murrell; collaborative Master Printer Frank Janzen,
published by Crow's Shadow Press (2012).*
20 21 22 23 24 5 4 3 2 1
First Edition

Milkweed Editions, an independent nonprofit publisher, gratefully acknowledges
sustaining support from the Alan B. Slifka Foundation and its president, Riva
Ariella Ritvo-Slifka; the Ballard Spahr Foundation; *Copper Nickel*; the Jerome
Foundation; the McKnight Foundation; the National Endowment for the Arts;
the National Poetry Series; the Target Foundation; and other generous contributions
from foundations, corporations, and individuals. Also, this activity is made possible
by the voters of Minnesota through a Minnesota State Arts Board Operating Support
grant, thanks to a legislative appropriation from the arts and cultural heritage fund.
For a full listing of Milkweed Editions supporters, please visit milkweed.org.

Library of Congress Cataloging-in-Publication Data

Names: Clay, Adam, 1978- author.
Title: To make room for the sea : poems / Adam Clay.
Description: First edition. | Minneapolis, Minnesota : Milkweed Editions,
    2020. | Identifiers: LCCN 2019041214 (print) | LCCN 2019041215 (ebook)
    | ISBN 9781571314970 (trade paperback ; alk. paper) | ISBN 9781571319722
    (ebook)
Subjects: LCGFT: Poetry.
Classification: LCC PS3603.L385 T62 2020 (print) | LCC PS3603.L385
    (ebook) | DDC 811/.6--dc23
LC record available at https://lccn.loc.gov/2019041214
LC ebook record available at https://lccn.loc.gov/2019041215

Milkweed Editions is committed to ecological stewardship. We strive to align our
book production practices with this principle, and to reduce the impact of our
operations in the environment. We are a member of the Green Press Initiative, a
nonprofit coalition of publishers, manufacturers, and authors working to protect
the world's endangered forests and conserve natural resources. *To Make Room for the
Sea* was printed on acid-free 30% postconsumer-waste paper by Versa Press.

Contents

And from growing dim, the coals
Fall alight. There are two ways to be.

—JOHN ASHBERY

Maybe you need to write a poem about grace.

—ROBERT HASS

TO MAKE

ROOM FOR

THE SEA

Good-bye to Golden Nights

If measuring
one's life circular
makes sense of movement,
then how should
we muscle meaning
into days? As if we end up
where we've dreamt,
starlight for eyes
and train whistles
within the folds
of memory. Then one story
arrives before another
ends, not rounded
with possibility
but carved down
to an orchestrated stutter.
We catch a glimpse
of self within the self.
Hope swims better than
it flies, arriving beneath
the smooth surface
of possibility with unseen
silent movement. No one
cares for the self
with as much bravado
as the mind, its expanse
opens like a shorn field
before the seed.

Last Anniversary

A few minutes inside the museum
made the sky lighten up,
as if we had a reason
to be there and we did,
though it wasn't
what you might expect:
a tercentenary off the balcony
in every direction
and down below: a tall ship,
another tall ship,
and a double-decker
swerving into traffic, too.
Back inside, an emergency exit
for each of us—
though the doorknobs
were taken off in a fit
of hope: perhaps
a worst-case scenario
won't arrive if we stay
unprepared for it, someone
thought they said out loud,
but they didn't and so
nothing much changed.
An early mockup design
of a fire extinguisher, guard rails
moved to a garden guiding
vines from the ground,
and a happy birthday for a city
as if anyone that many years back
would have imagined
our collective imagination,
our unending desire

for the dramatic. Most of those
paintings we saw that day
were puzzles that hadn't been cut
into a thousand pieces yet.

Mississippi Elegy

The real wilderness is not out
there—it's in here, deep inside
the quick run of blood. Every day

I consider what going home means
now that I'm here again:
I make a list of what settles the mind,

a list of what floats through a sky
filled with trees from this vantage point:
Slash and Shortleaf, Loblolly and Longleaf.

We pass by them daily, not thinking
of what they carry within their long memory.
If *Death makes equals of us all,* then why

does the ground reveal an answer
only to what goes unspoken? I know the answer,
but I don't let it enter the room. Beneath

every question is an elegy, and beneath
every elegy lives the promise that a life
will persist long after its song.

Go Birding

Daylight ran short.
When'd the moon

show up? said someone
and then everyone. Inside

now the ocean feels a tug,
and the greenery

nailed to the door
stays green

long past its prime,
expiration date expired.

One could inject
anything into

the small talk
of evening, but what

can't be taken back
is the breath taken

with no thought.
Every sky turns

its back at last, no
applause needed. One

only demands that which
can't couple for nothing.

How Do You Feel about Ashbery?

What's more central than beginning with a question,
like *how many trees at minimum comprise an orchard?*
or *why is my password outdated in its quaintness?* Two
dead dogs and a holiday named for the planet
we don't deserve. That's your hint. I farm thoughts
from stray feelings like they'll rush out temporarily
and beat some rhythm no human ear's ever curved
around. Why say *thank you* when there's no need
for gratitude mingled with intention? I had put love into
each action and what became overgrown wasn't intention,
but how to blame the specific for growing more obscure

than some twisted version of itself? Like a face
I had never seen, its creasing sent me elsewhere
so easily. Mornings seem longer these days, the biscuits
stick to the pan long past noon, maybe even into next year.
Why glance toward what we expect? There's more sense
in the unfamiliar stars we chart our lives by, following their
paths like what's lived is right out of reach. My body
lumbers to light as if that's what it should turn to
and why shouldn't it? No one's counting down the days
but you and I—it's easy to be forgotten in the act of undoing,
but no shadow's left by a ghostly action. I have a thousand
things to say right before my heart seizes up,

a muscle braided and turned tighter. It's sensible
to perceive the unexpected. Everything's improbable,
after all. In private we find less of an echo and a more
true and real version of the self. No stitches showing: an event
with an asterisk by it or a bloom golden right before
the flower dies. I cited your towering wisdom before
you gave it to me and found quirks in the most normal

of conversations, like how an instant felt less cosmic
and more like a coffee spoon wound around the mug,
un-useable, its purpose redesigned. Hard not to wonder

what trial will teach the trees to rise up, to eventually
know how we've aligned ourselves with lives
outside our own. Nothing worth the weight of a star
lifts the eye like your face waiting for wonder.
It's true. I've arrived in this body how many times
on the other end of sleep? A day drifts away
if you let it be torn from the calendar, ripped
from the memory you misremembered into two halves
or maybe three parts, now that you think of it. Time
is less pregnant with meaning, though. It's too early
to limit the path of my thinking, as if the security of light
could be dangerous if I let it. So I don't. What's unknown
in the future feels more sensible than the past, but I'll
trust what can't be seen before I trust the small houses
still lit up with memories from the night before.

Meditation for the Silence of Morning

I wake myself imagining the shape
of the day and where I will find

myself within it. Language does not
often live in that shape,

but sentences survive somehow
through the islands of dark matter,

the negative space often more important
than the positive.

Imagine finding you look at the world
completely different upon waking one day

and not knowing if this version is permanent.
Anything can change, after all,

for how else would you find yourself
in this predicament or this opportunity,

depending on the frame? A single moment
can make loneliness seem frighteningly new.

We destroy the paths of rivers
to make room for the sea.

At the Heart of a Multitude of Things

A settlement rises up with an intertwined sense
of both respect and fear for the world sprawling
around it. Some go to the wild looking for
an answer to silence, while others end up
not knowing how they've managed to arrive
there to begin with. Eventually, this notion vanishes

into the fog like only a mountain can vanish:
one day an object to build a life around and next: the sense
of its shape gone like a rabbit, as quickly as it arrived.
What replaces the irreplaceable? Some sprawling
invasive vine? Some myth from the night brought up
like a solid fact? What should a life be for,

if not for opening these questions, if not for
where the self ends and the world's varnish
rubs off on one's view? Being dreamt up
by the darkness suggests the sense
of where one has come from, of how sprawling
starts slowly, like how a thousand arrivals

can end with a single departure. This arrival
isn't meant to be literal. A year or four
go by so quickly while a minute sprawls
like a day. How to sum up this vanishing
that falls through the branches with a sense
only some strange god might have thought up

in a drunken stumble? Why bother rising up
against an accidental start? Better to have arrived
than to have not? There's a fumbling sense
of hope, a tiny branch dropped in the ocean for

the long float toward land. The sky will vanish
over the horizon, and the stars sprawling

over the sky will eventually sprawl
over the rubble of what was thought up
only to slowly fall away, only to vanish
with such perfection that its sudden arrival
must be accepted with a long slow nod, for
it couldn't have been any other way. Sense

and its long forgotten order sums up
a certain lack of sense, a plant meant to sprawl,
arrive miles from root, break its form, and vanish.

Only Child (III)

In these months of rethinking, one wonders
where to find rest again. Where in a moment
is the music of a dying leaf? In another
life there was time to listen, but in this one
I find there's only time to leave some subtle
message for my child. A few blocks over
a piano plays some nonsense by itself.

Found in Translation

What starts off as nihilistic
inside the folds of my thinking

usually ends up as stray
unkempt optimism. Not a happy accident,

but more a blur of accidental happiness
smudged with a tone I can't quite name.

It's evening, and I number how many
unread books remain unwritten,

marvel at what the body will do
to survive. To delay the inevitable

can seem heroic under some
circumstances, reckless under others.

Did you see the Appaloosa in the sky?
A horse made of clouds? No, it was a horse

turning into two horses. What were they doing?
I don't know. There was one for each eye.

How the World Began

The years of the locust tree
split open with ease,
but I had no ax—
it was lost to the snow.
Let's make up a story
of how we arrived here.
Because of its ability to create,
the mind must do the opposite.
I always liked missing you,
stirring the coals with only
the action of my mind.
To split wood, one must consider
the direction of the grain.
Sometimes these mornings
remind me of how
Dickinson imagined heaven,
but what of heaven
without the world, the dirt,
and the turn of the head
to a sound distant and now
near in the woods? I doubt
anything could diminish
the seasons when dwelling
within the opposite. How we
arrived here was never much
of a story, but yet we imagined
a path around the lake,
a narrative built from circumference,
and the trees we built
from molecules outgrew the shallow
bounds we imagined for them.

The Seams Don't Show

A cloud fills the sky trying to convey importance to an otherwise
backward-looking day. Most moments are pieces to a puzzle

cut so the seams don't show, but it's best to ignore the day's
dripping faucet, the saucer missing its cup. There's a need for

energy to be harnessed into an idea, but in the wild, what
forgotten life should we thread out once we find the spirit

gone from this life? What we want becomes replaced by
high windows you can't clean and nothing to see but light

inside the dark corners of the rooms you've left behind.
Just now I find myself caught in the folds of a sentence

kindness forgot. What can be taken back? Nothing. Best
let go of it for now. We judge a point in time by other points

missed by opportunity, and we usually stop finding the universe
new by afternoon. You've looked out the door each morning

only to find the view's changed little over time, but life feels
passive and grows more so the further you go from the bed,

quietly unsure of what the day holds. As if moving through the day
repeats a pattern from another point in time, the bees keep their

sight on a task and find temper in the heat of their movement.
Tacitly they form a new sense of silence. What else would you expect

unearthed from the little buzzing impulse within them and you and me?
Very easy to think of *us* as a *we*, but that's not quite right. In actuality,

what I mean: the stars glowed golden long before even
xerothermic times. In imagining a color for the first time,

you'd need a word for the shade, too. This wasn't meant for the star
zigzagging from the sky. It's gone like it wasn't ever there at all.

Now Warm and Capable

—for Max Ritvo

Before sleep, I hear the wind chimes
from our neighbors' front porch
and backyard and from

the other side of their house. The chimes
make some kind of sense of the wind,

though I don't know what sense
it might be. For beauty only?
Or a sieve for the chaos to slip through?

The week before last Ada asked Michael and I
if we believed in God, a higher power,

a whatever. A few months back Richie
posited that search engine histories
have become the closest thing

to prayer we have. I don't know why origins
mean so much to us,

and why our unknowing must sting like a scar.
The way we reckon depends on the day's shade.
Think of the sweet spire and how you might

miss the native if you aren't looking for it, as if
each day finds its ending in a homily of undoing.

Understories

1.

A patch of leaves furrows
the treetop

from ethereal to solid
while its base hollows in the sun.

2.

What alphabet
these grounded twigs

will arrive at

depends on the wind
and what its billowing

urges to be said.

Say *patient* for impatiens,
say *willow* for oak,

say observation
is the kindest of all actions.

3.

I don't know which air feels more buoyant,
that which gathers along the crest of the hill

or the air finding its way through
the beak of the blue-winged warbler.

4.

The inside of the trees seem like understories
to their leaves.

Dependence frames most equations.

No need for the honesty of the ax
to know what you already should say.

5.

A branch does not require Herculean greatness,
but the tree does it anyway.

Somewhere ants parachute, aloft
with their lack of intention. Where they land,
the narrative need not notice.

6.

The crow mocks the ant's short life from afar.

Its brief movement creates a demented Z,
suggesting a purposed indifference.

Meanwhile the river meanders downhill
to a creek and a river again.

Its movement moves away from metaphor.

7.

From one side, the tree-seed shell mirrors a split cranium.
From the other, a hedgehog crouching roadside-ready.

8.

In formation, the birds walk in circles
each wing tucked in like a knuckle.

9.

Beyond the point of human reflection,
the mind turns to creosote before it turns to fragments.

10.

The arborist has submitted her
official resignation

to the gods of air and weightlessness.

They open another bottle of wine, drop
the cork into the darkest part of the sea.

11.

Say anything is rife with gravity—
the planet skitters over its own cracked beauty.

In Bed and Where Is the Sun?

End of January
and a single bird

sings once
outside the window,

a rectangle to see
the fragments

of the world through.
What of the pieces

that turn to air alone,
but become

something of heft
all together? I think of

Keats and his bed burning
with fever, then

consumed by flame
after. Ornamental

we all manage to be,
but what to do with a fact

isn't always the same:
the bird sang once

and went away. The morning
is a place for quiet,

its breathing sometimes
too slow to measure.

Acre, Heather, Square

On one side
of the metaphor
you find a house
while on the other,
the view remains blocked
from sight, eyes pushed
into another sense
of light. Go on. Ask
the question of yesterday
in the light of today.
Like describing
an empty field with
only three words,
there's no point
in hovering over
absence so directly.
Instead, clouds appear
casting shadows,
and the question
becomes not how
to describe the field
but rather is the field
now empty? No rain.
The clouds fragment
off into layers of blue air.

For a Turtle Eating a Strawberry

Life mostly feels like walking the line
between an elegy and an ode,

between fierce love and fierceness
boiled down to a rock,

tossed into some lake in the mind
with the purpose only creation

can contain. How
not to let the mind think

what would happen
if the path reversed,

if we floated from the water,
love and loss braided endlessly

together? And it's easy
to say: *it must be us,*

it must be the human mind,
but it can't be so simple. I am taking

this morning apart,
so call this poem what you will—I'll keep

the name of the world to myself.
It's easier to love what we don't know.

A Joke about How Old We've Become

I take a break from the morning's work
to pay a credit card bill,
to take the dog out, to water

the plants in the hanging baskets,
but why not instead take a walk
through the early August morning

before the heat wave hits? The body's
still stretching itself out. The music goes
from minor to major when you flip

the album, but sometimes
the minor starts over before you cross
the room, and sometimes it's best

to just listen, best to not fill
any space with words.
The stars and the stripes catch

the eye more so than the blank space,
like a life to be filled up with
something bigger than breath. My dad

last night on the phone told me
the tests came back positive
but not to worry, but how

not to worry with his almost three decades
ahead of me, and what is a year
really when they pile up, time to dust

the furniture again, to check
on the slow-draining sink,
clean it out, start the day with a list

of what a day should even mean
or be, not minding how fast the hours go by
until eventually I will, which by then it will

be too late, though I do not mean
my life means anything in the scheme
of stepping back we all do, chipping

at some unmovable block of rock,
as if time won't eventually
undo even its looming shape too.

Blue Screen of Death

Today I wonder who
moved the high steeples
of my childhood, knowing

there's a twist at the end
of the answer because the urge
to dig deeper is coded somewhere

cold within the folds of my
past lives. What other animal
would teach a computer

to be a Buddhist, to design itself
right out of existence with this much
hubris? The sea somewhere

feels gnarled but not here,
not now. Enlightenment might
be the only gift we could

even give. In our effort the bricks
were set so carefully, we can't see
the source or shape of the light.

Of course there's a candle
that doesn't burn out, but no one
knows how to light it.

Only Child (II)

Life finds its way into the cracks
of the world like water and how

to put rushing water into words? How
the body replaces a body like a clock

breaking down and catching again
a few seconds behind. I first held my child

not knowing what I was doing. Now
she stretches like grain to the sky.

Ghazal for a Farewell Transmission

The line between public and personal? It depends on the world.
I know this poem should be no place for the violent acts of the world.

Forgive me. After Sandy Hook, I felt fear curl like a fern
in each corner's edge, wondered where we cease to shape our world.

Half the mass in our bodies traveled from outside the galaxy, the other
half from our own, as if to explain the pull we feel to another world.

I think most days of how *we will be gone but not forever*, and I write down
one memory a day, as if an image can contain a changing world.

What did the president say to the day which should have no words?
I don't know. I turned the radio off, steered left into a static world.

How a tree responds to injury I heard days before. It creates a barrier
zone. It does not heal. It seals itself off from the world.

My daughter was in the back seat of the car. I saw her face reflecting
each atom within me. Life is a fact aligned with our sense of the world.

The Terror of Flight

Good morning mess of stars
just out of sight
and other things we make

invisible with the promise
of their design. Reflections
may chisel a strange song,

but think of skin
worn down under
the mass of

panic (or purpose)
and not the trajectory
of missile fire scarring

the sky. Why must "missile"
contain the word "miss," as if built
into its horror is the assurance

it will land where it
wasn't meant to? Think of a pointed
word or a smoothed stone

purposed for disaster. History
waits for everyone or for
no one, and a shawl covers

only what's a thumb smaller
than itself. Drifting from
the skyscraper in my mind, its pattern

billows and opens, falling along
and further down like a flag
bereft of its pole so gently it flails.

America

In the painting
of a painting,
there's little
to be said
of sadness,
as if opening up
within itself
is a way of
misremembering
personal history.
I remember
the museum
where the painting
was shown,
its walls so full
their colors
were obscured
from the eye.
When the soldiers
arrived, it
was like any
other installation:
strange in its
existence, changing
the way a frame
has its own life
free from its art,
the walls divided
as if being torn down.

State of the Union

The morning's just getting started
as the citizens haul their trash out to the curb.
Why shouldn't they piece their lives together
based on what they no longer have a use for?
Likely there's some version of hope or comfort
found within each simple slow ritual,

but what to make of life when there's no ritual
worth praising? Sometimes even starting
to think of an inevitable void is a comfort
we keep for ourselves, a minor way of curbing
the mind from danger. What else could it be for?
A brief notion of what it means to be together?

The citizens stop at the streets as if tethered
to their homes. To be considered a ritual,
one ponders repetition and why four
follows three on the tongue before five starts
its sound. Looking further past the curb
now, the citizens turn back to the comfort

of their small homes. But what should comfort
be in the face of loneliness? Hope huddled together
with other stray ideas? Eventually these long curbs
set against the street will be moved: one ritual
shifts into another like how each day starts
and finishes with dark. What else should twenty-four

hours, with their constant slipping away, exist for?
The state of the union is constant discomfort
couched in the illusion of promise. One may start
to look inward, but the notion of working together

does not always assume the slow pace of ritual.
The citizens kick their best hopes to the curb

with everything else. They would get rid of the curbs,
too, if it wasn't easier to keep lines in place for
what they suggest: a physical ritual
meant to provide a minor sense of comfort
in a dark time. Looking through glass together
does not diminish solitude, nor does it start

to curb a lack of desire for something more. To start
movement forward or to start movement together
toward an empty ritual does little but refuse comfort.

My Thought Is Only a Mirror for Yours

—aft. N. S.

Dry mud south from my words and a thought cast: did I
bury my body? My off/on switch missing, no way to drop
skin in this post-world as if in a bold mouth

a word for that word might

find for its synonym: *cosmos.* Gossip of sick
royalty at risk, what option but to ask for turnaround,
not for royalty only, but for humans

who would find mounds of dirt thrown on skin

and his royal blood. A man in my past coos still
of what's crumbling, did, and a laugh
for him. What twists to crumbs will vanish

in a vacuum and quickly

for it only. Land for our living, loving
and untrusting clan, what was around:
goldmarks only upon dying, but not its bonds of dirt—

Form of Love

I always think that I can manage the highest form of love.
—ANGELA BALL

I've always been a painter
with no talent for painting,
no patience for blurring
color or for putting
the marble blue in my mind
down on a canvas cold
with promise. My mind
holds the past too well
and not well enough
at the same time, some
strange purgatory dreamt
by a god that never had time
for time's passing. It's these
things, yes, but it's also
the thought of the audience
in the gallery, the onlookers
alive now and those that aren't
born yet; it's this audience
in particular that slows the
the impulse I feel but cannot
name. How willful must one
be to stop the body from enacting
the mind? A mistake made
and forgotten makes its luster
streak silvery, perfect,
and new each time.

Just Off a Highway in North Central Missouri

To drive across a state so as to change
the weather from
a purple henbit unfolding
into a train that circles back onto itself,
its path leading to the question
of how many rivers one can cross
in a single day.
In our implicit design, we are meant
to lose count,
and in this fault we find acceptance
for we see too easily
where the mind travels to,
not like the mouse
with its lack of foresight:
one moment here
and in another
it flies above and beyond
to a slab of concrete a hundred miles
from what might as well
be another star. And then:
a blink and another droning
from the wind pushing against the force
of the hand: a shifting
without feeling of darkness
or kindness. If right now
I were to break into anything,
it would be those trees lining the field
looking nearly dead, for in their
rickety limbs there lies a promise
too great for even the wrong season
to take away, too great
for even the strongest wind to maim.

Elsewhere

A bear makes the sea part of the basement.
But that's elsewhere. Every day someone goes
to the post office and doesn't mail

anything. I wish I was dreaming of coal mines
filled with rock again, but this coffee glows
as dark as the day seems to be. The birds

in the trees are not real, but they call out
anyhow, and the song seems just right for the haze
of October and the glue that holds us together.

The edges blur a bit after lunch, but I can
still make out what needs to be done, needs to be
said. I'm too tired to think of chains as metal. The birth

of a child on the day you will die isn't something
to think of ahead of your passing, but in that moment
we'll all welcome the missing patterns of rain.

Immortality for Mary Ruefle

I don't often disagree, but today I mouth the idea: *you will live forever*. This impulse finds its way into every moment of every day, so routine it fills the iron with water, it erases wrinkled clothes and skin while you sleep. I know your body is not weightless in water— which is admittedly odd—but when the dust of stars formed your mind, it happened so quickly that your immortality was hidden by unworldly things, not the water collecting on a thorny flower or the seeds dropped from the height of the tree that could cure this illness called *life*. You're always on the clock, and not even time can be measured as you move through particles of matter that hold some ancestor you couldn't think to channel. Everyone wants this gift except for you. There was no sense in etching your name in the tree, but you did it anyway.

The Art That We Are

—*after Alice Notley*

I like the thought of an afterlife
void of feelings, all types of sadness
gone missing, perhaps swept
to some strange otherworld for
shaded abstractions, stunted ideas,
the slightest of thoughts, and untested
concepts. *It's nice to be stuck in traffic,*
is not a sentence you hear often,
but near death, I imagine
being grateful for those thirty minutes
stalled an hour or so out of that city
I'll never see again in this life.
An experience without feeling
or a feeling without experience?
I choose neither. I fashion each
fleeting thought into a tiny lead boat.

When the Whale Becomes the Wave

Within the confines of metaphor, the florist
drives the same route to work daily, sunshine
melting to perfect flakes of snow. Ultimately
we must manufacture our own importance.
Without much guidance, I learned at an early age
that time defines most of our words and actions
with a tinge of terrible and calm perfection.
The ocean does one thing well—if it were you
or I, it'd be called *stuck*. And gravity seems
level on the surface: a train married to its parallel
tracks. But look deeper: we don't mean to talk
to ourselves when we talk to ourselves, but no one
listens the way we do. If words could be worth
more than their meaning, I'd believe colors—and not just
their names—were capable of great and greater things.

Where the Map Is

No word for the snow you didn't see pile up too quick for the eye to measure, but there's something to be said for the second between taking in a vision and processing it. It isn't pure light, but it's the next best thing, the only loving path through the mind to another type of mind, The Walkmen covering Nilsson who covered Dylan. Not what Plato had imagined in his time, but there's always a specific way to feel homesick, a way to chart a path to loneliness without knowing its sort or its source. I used to think a mosaic was how best to describe an urge devout in one light and profane in another, looking inward before chiseling a way out.

What Shines Does Not Always Need To

Because today we did not leave this world,
we now embody a prominence within it,
even amidst its indifference to our actions,
whether noiseless or not. After all,
nonsense is its own type of silence, lasting
as long as the snow on your tongue. She asked
why each evening should be filled with a turning
away, eyes to the lines of the hardwood floor
as if to regret the immobility of a single day, our callous
hope for another wish put to bed with the others
in a slow single-file line. I used to be amazed
at the weight an ant could carry. I used to be surprised
by survival. But now I know the mind can carry
itself to the infinite power. Like the way snow
covers trauma to the land below it, we only
believe the narrative of what the eye can see.

Watching You Make Dinner

This room needs our bodies
less than we need the room.
There's always something
to guard against, to hold up
between the thought
of two bodies touching
or breaking or broken. Outside
the dark feels more civilized
than the animal urge
to walk off toward the horizon
I know is there, but I can't
see. We feel one way
before we feel another.

Fall Bird

The cardinal looked
nuclear at a distance—

the red line across
my view split vision

from thinking, left
an intention I'd need

to somehow walk
straight through. A circle

traced long enough
turns to a square.

Exile

There is night and there is night,
though neither are good or bad.
A mark of punctuation through
the face—a slash, I think, like how
the reality of breathing means less
than how we do it. Deeply
in a debt of feelings always, how
to bicycle to work in the rain and show
up dry and happy not like a tick
stuffed on blood, but a lion starved
after week upon week of animal
loneliness? It wasn't a slash; it
was an exclamation point
void of enthusiasm, a failed
attempt at willing a person back
to life. I'm carried away so much
these days the smallest gust could
pick me up, set me down
in a new town, with a new face,
a new pattern of shapes.

Finding Yourself in a Museum Gallery

To match the background
the eye destroys the foreground,
develops the idea of afternoon
into an evening wrecked
slowly into a form
the mind eventually recognizes
until sleep. A blue sky blooms
unreal—it needs watering you'd like
to think, but it doesn't
wash away its memory so easily,
as simple as time's gravel
wearing down even itself
as if to recognize your face
on a foreign wall is to recognize
a thought you never had.
This is an experience
everyone will have at least
once in their lifetime, maybe
twice. What to do with
the moments that dumbfound
us with awe? No removal
or distance is enough to tear
the sky into sense
so you become part of it
for a moment, the child
with the face of an animal
walking away from the viewer
toward the place where all lines
go, a sharp emphatic point, the gray
thunder of everyone's last thought.

No Longer Yours

Never mind the sky refusing to drop away.
What we hold firmly in the past, the present
will always resist, like how petals hold on
because their future depends on it. In the woods
of today, the brown light cuts the sky
crisply with violence. No one knows what
to call water when it rips through a living thing,
leaving smelt and mold behind. Frost falls
like another thing altogether
with the apple of an idea meaning little as it rots
outside the house built on a pond fed
by a creek that went dry overnight. What breaks
the day into parts doesn't need a name
or a hill to be placed upon where dying becomes
ideal in some deep sense. To stare
at the black sky until it turns brown
takes from the woods what it held
uninterrupted in its *gray trunk of trees.*
Any trauma takes the blue from the bluet
and sets the focus down mundanely,
finds a moment of spring in fall, not as if
unexpected, but rather coldly anticipated
and written off by someone tearing pages
from a book in the woods the pulp came from.
Anyone can write anything, but to read
a line out loud means it is no longer yours.
It means it has broken light, changed color,
flowered into something larger than itself. Late
and late, a single bluet finds a way to survive.

Broken Form

You have to look at it as one person
with a very long life
it's better that way
—MARY RUEFLE

There's a way grief slows time,
but what slows grief like fruit
rotting on the counter, soap stuck
in the drain? I'm looking for ancestral
knowledge in the brain of a child,
and sometimes I find it, and sometimes
I hold the word *wonder* up to the light
like a new species of blackberry
that disappears when I close my eyes.
I once thought of difference as deferring
an impulse into another, but what
god would one pray to if religions
weren't filled with faults of their own?
I know the strange sob gasping
in and out from the other room
will cease eventually. I pray to the body
and its broken final form.

Sonnet

There's a point between   being and not
that becomes a twisted type of life—

The knot's tied and untied with each breath

To find the world *believe* startling at the end
of a line   To find a river conscious
        and aware of itself

What of the rock that contains another rock
It decides fate   without being asked

A new word   for the same age
Why not drift through gold to land in silence

I knew something was off
something usual   so unusual

The brain splits itself in moments of grief
What feels like light   becomes ash instead

Taken Off the Bone

Like a strange thing at night, these moments
garble clearly through the heart
of what matters and what storms suddenly. Danger
like a point of safety for others, as if blood
spilled can also be blood saved. Happiness?
Some strange sort of forever
or whatever—like the time number you'd
call to set your clock to. Thought
and thoughtlessness seem braided today,
then unstitched eventually, transfigured
into something secular, something happiness
replaces at times. No explanation, just a vanishing.

Domestic Barbarians

A prayer to the void makes more sense
than a prayer to the dirty dishes
tossed to the trash, the trash
tossed to the yard, piles of leaves
rising to kill the grass
beneath them. Each day's a failure,
but failures accumulate into
something substantial. I feel
most sure of myself when
I'm suspicious of myself. Perhaps
we're gods among
the debris of our living.

Only Child (I)

Breakfast rained on again,
and I'm lifted up the stairs
on the breath of what
the dark of the day
might promise in its
early silence. The light of my
daughter's room has been
on all night like every night,
but the sun shifting
changes the shape
of the space from
a square into an unfolding
universe. I had always
imagined a different type
of fatherhood before
fatherhood found me, but if you
asked me to describe it now,
I don't think I could
find the words. Try to find
a way to describe living
a few different ways at once.
For a while I imagined
there would be more attempts
at trying out what I'm still
trying to see in the room
that's gone power out,
but the weeds in the yard
grow too quickly to be left
alone for long. I had forgotten
the strangeness of a humid
February. I had forgotten
all that makes up the memories

that need me to exist. It was
easier to carve out a place
before I had words to describe
it. Now looking back feels
like looking forward. It isn't
a mistake to see wreckage
before it happens. I am
drawing a self-portrait
and trying to remove the self.

Uncovered at the Falls

1.

But it's January, and I think it's a bee. No matter—
your prized thought is a star hung strangely in the sky,
a saucer of light reflecting mistakes
retold, maybe even a dinner party of families, and it's time
to rethink what the word *family* even means. I'm designing
new forms of kindness, but the self always
needs something more, doesn't it? The boats beached
here believe in water so surely I'd sign up for a naval
commitment without knowing the destination.
On another note, I like how you describe the mundane
in nuclear terms—I'd like to be with you in the afterlife
and a touch before, too, though I'd never
think of shadows the same way. My dreams
confuse people and situations so routinely. I hear
running water above the buzz of electrical
humming, but this life seems intent on shuffling
its cards, and among the metaphors
I'm dividing time like those crickets
we first heard together in the future—I'll squeeze
your hand in that moment: know that.

2.

It's not a new day here (so many shadows!),
and I'm wallowing in the fact of the brown grass
and how it seems so much surer than the sky.
It's funny how the word *like* creates
an entire world in the mind, a world I'd be okay
with if you forgot the previous afterlife, water steeping

on the stove like a routine, a stone that's always
been there (see what I did just then?). It makes sense
to fall back into memory, perhaps the deepest
channel dug but not always so terrible. I'd like to reshape
most of what you say into a question tossed
toward the light of morning, just to see
what you'd say to your mind reframed
in different words or different verbs,
and that distant point is a lonesome thought
lit up with hope. Let's warm our hands
by the fire, imagining how our faces look in its light
to one another, knowing full well I'd give
you a year of my life if you could describe
my expression in five words or less. I'm ready.

Confluence of Objects

Radio turned from static
to news of a storm approaching

and worsening but then:
no—it's a star passing

across the night sky, moving too fast
to be anything cosmic

except for the star stretching out
to nothing everyone saw but you,

but then you *do* see one
but it's most likely not a star

and how strange to look up and out
for how many million miles

and not see what's just below
your body in the water,

how strange to hear the instrument
pluck of the bullfrog's croak

from somewhere to the northwest
or the southeast and not know which

and yes in this blanket form of night
the eye matches image to sense pausing

on what memory finds an urge
to catalogue, but not actually

because the mind is its own star,
its own object both anchored

to and aloft in the night sky,
burning not fuel but a memory

of what's past due or forgotten
for the sake of convenience, of finding

a rare flower in a field of grass,
of rows of corn that carried

and will carry a bright morning star,
of finding an unnamed fire in the sky,

but *no* is an arrival because the names
we write down for what we see

will only matter for a moment, lucky
confluence of objects our bodies are,

for the self is always on its way toward
a place where collective memory

will be no memory at all, and yes it means
less to mistake the light of the sky

with the objects overhead because mistaking
an object for another is the sense of the mind

working itself out or rather it's a quarry
to be mined, and to be left for nature to fix

or is it *quarry* as a verb or most likely a path
through two fields, past a dark house,

the tongue held to preserve the silence,
a prayer for the oldest worlds within us.

And Late . . .

. . . or not but always on time (a gift
from my father: *if you're on time*

you're late) because
there's no way really

to define *early*
in that even a minute

isn't measurable
enough when you're waiting

or wanting which
means: arriving early

means being alone a touch more.
In a poem not about punctuality,

Joe Brainard says: *I think it's always*
nice to know you are not

alone. Even in death. And maybe
thinking of death as a destination

is better than dreading
what's to come. We are here for

a little blink, and then
we'll be together for a long while.

If I Could Write Small Enough, These Words Would Fit on the Back of a Postcard

I'm stopped by my stubbed toe on the watercolor pavement,
but more importantly I'm stuck in a sentence I can't
quite remember. It's one I've said in a circle
so many times. A bicycle shoved into the backseat,
a bass guitar still in tune fifteen years at this decade's end.
It's as tall as my daughter, and she's happy to strum the thumping
strings and laugh at what music it might have held. Where's
the amp now? I remember dropping it from a height because
a short distance felt impossible. Who was I? Where's my face
blurring up from the memories I still contain? Is that all one's
life is? Or would flowers we imagine crowd over those we
can see? I'm sorry. On the edge of a highway we passed that day
nothing seemed worthy of lineation. I'm in the kitchen, I'm in
the backyard. I'm inside again. In every action there's an equal
and impossible subtraction. I wish a wooden chair screeching
across the floor could be how this all ends (and how tidy it would be),
but it won't, and I'm glad most conclusions feel like bees working
on a task the careful and close logic of our minds just can't see.

For Broken Things

Wonder — is not precisely knowing
And not precisely knowing not
—EMILY DICKINSON

No love for the outdoors
more than I love this drifting

February spring day with
a distilling sense of ennui

for a different sort of gulf, not this
Midwestern prairie or the way

a room changes shape
because of what it

contains. I don't feel tempted
to shove this sadness away,

but I haven't yet stepped
outside of the confines

of my lineated mind today. What
was a year ago, I ask my phone,

and it tells me mistakes
are okay which is what my daughter

was thinking two years back
during a craft talk

Natalie was giving to my students
about poems, their sense,

and their lack of it, too. I took notes
that day, but that notebook

is where? I don't know.
My phone also tells me

three years back
I was reminded of Dickinson

on wonder, though
I don't know what

took me there or where I went
from her words, maybe like a dash

from her mind into another thought
but more likely toward a cup of coffee

I've long since forgotten too.
Back in the present,

Brian writes to me that aliens
would from a distant point

see our data centers
as the dominant life form

on our warming planet,
and they would imagine

us to be nothing more than
worker bees populating cells

while their fans pull sense
from every question better left

unasked. When I think to elegize
the broken or the forgotten,

I am mourning the self from a week
back, a year, or maybe even

a dozen now. It's a miracle to forget
and a shame sometimes we don't. Natalie

writes in a poem that "Whatever [she]
cares for, someone

else loves it more, deserves it more"
[line breaks are mine, with apologies],

and I think about being left
alone on an island

with no recollection
of society,

asking what love
would even mean without

the love of others. These words
this moment are a record of how

I'm embracing a single ounce of wonder
for the way it sharpens

my heart into a perfect fit,
into a stumbling mess of stars.

In Praise of Unknowing

—for Cate Peebles

What's a gift really? I knew
nothing of New Haven,
but you told me how wind

unearths bodies from
The Green, forcing the trees
to give up their grip on the soil.

How many things to know
or to not learn? Or how many
to unlearn? I hold this leaf I think

you should see, but I can't quite
say why. Mostly we can't choose
what we learn, but we

can learn to decide what we'll
do with knowledge or time
or weather. What do I know

of myself? The thousand
lives I've lived before this one
say more at times than

the immediacy of any present
moment. Penny told me last night
she's afraid of clowns, vintage dolls,

and the color brown. I didn't
tell her about a dream I've had
since childhood, flying low

across the ground or maybe
a structure of some sort,
with a shade of brown leaves

from some tree stuck in my
throat. I have no words for
how I feel in the dream,

no narrative I can
pin to the inner corner
of its image. Before the leaves

had fallen a few months back,
I thought this new life was ash
and fire, but what if it was a view into

a world I hadn't envisioned yet,
a world I'm only now starting to see?
What's a gift, really? Its identity

exists in the unknown
blurs and shades of improbability.
I am forty years old and just realized

I barely know myself and those
around me, but how much
hope lives within the fact

of what's to come? The leaves fall
up toward the sky. For every oak
tree fallen, let's plant two more.

Acknowledgments

Thank you to the editors of the following journals in which some of these poems first appeared: The Academy of American Poets' Poem-a-Day Project, *The Believer* (online), *Bennington Review, Crazyhorse, Denver Quarterly, Descant, Exit 7, Georgia Review, Grist, jubilat, Laurel Review, Los Angeles Review, Pinwheel, Poet's Country, Poetry Northwest, Tin House, Seneca Review,* and *The Shallow Ends.* This manuscript was completed thanks to the generous support of a Literary Artist Fellowship from the Mississippi Arts Commission.

Thank you to my colleagues in the Center for Writers at the University of Southern Mississippi: Angela Ball, Joshua Bernstein, and Olivia Clare. Thank you to the students at USM. I'm also grateful to the instructors and students at the *Kenyon Review* Young Writers Workshop. Thank you to Claire Oleson for the first line of "Elsewhere."

Thank you Jericho Brown, Maggie Smith, Traci Brimhall, Abby Travis, Patrick Thomas, and Chris Martin.

I'm forever grateful to everyone at Milkweed Editions, especially Joey McGarvey, Mary Austin Speaker, Daniel Slager, Joanna Demkiewicz, Lee Oglesby, Jordan Bascom, Shannon Blackmer, and Bailey Hutchinson.

Thank you especially to Michael Robins, Ada Limón, Monika Gehlawat, Natalie Shapero, Hanif Abdurraqib, Autumn McClintock, and Cate Peebles.

This book is for Penny Clay.

Lucas Marquardt

ADAM CLAY is the author of three collections of poems: *Stranger, A Hotel Lobby at the Edge of the World,* and *The Wash.* His poems have appeared in *Tin House, Ploughshares, Denver Quarterly, Georgia Review, Crazyhorse, Bennington Review,* and *jubilat,* and online at Poetry Daily and the Poem-a-Day project of the Academy of American Poets. He is editor of *Mississippi Review,* a coeditor of *Typo Magazine,* and a book review editor for *Kenyon Review.* He teaches in the Center for Writers at the University of Southern Mississippi.

milkweed
editions

Founded as a nonprofit organization in 1980,
Milkweed Editions is an independent publisher. Our mission
is to identify, nurture and publish transformative literature,
and build an engaged community around it.

milkweed.org

Interior design by Mary Austin Speaker
Typeset in Bembo

Bembo was created in the 1920s under the direction
of printing historian Stanley Morison for the Monotype
Corporation. Bembo is based upon the 1495 design cut by
Francesco Griffo for Aldus Manutius, and named after the first
book to use the typeface, a small book called *De Aetna*, by the
Italian poet and cleric Pietro Bembo.